VIRAT KOHLI

JUGGERNAUT BOOKS
C-I-128, First Floor, Sangam Vihar, Near Holi Chowk,
New Delhi 110080, India

First published by Juggernaut Books 2025

Copyright © Harismita Vaideswaran 2025

10 9 8 7 6 5 4 3 2 1

P-ISBN: 9789353454517
E-ISBN: 9789353453985

The views and opinions expressed in this book are the author's own. The facts contained herein were reported to be true as on the date of publication by the author to the publishers of the book, and the publishers are not in any way liable for their accuracy or veracity.

All rights reserved. No part of this publication may be reproduced, transmitted or stored in a retrieval system in any form or by any means without the written permission of the publisher.

Typeset in Futura Std by R. Ajith Kumar, Noida

Printed at Thomson Press India Ltd

*For Amma
Who's always driven me to do it all,
and do it well.*

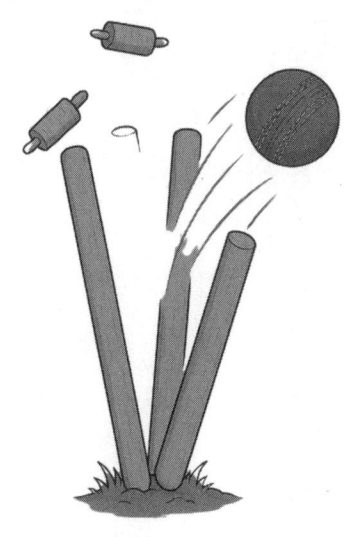

CONTENTS

1. King Fit for a Kohli — 1
2. Where It All Began — 13
3. Salad Days — 27
4. When the Light Shifts — 39
5. The Cup of the World — 57
6. The Coronation of Captain Kohli — 67
7. One Great Knock — 85
8. What's a Crown to a King? — 99
9. Kohli Fit for a King — 109
10. Virat Kohli: The Man — 117
11. Epilogue — 127

1
KING FIT FOR A KOHLI

The crowd sounds like it's baying for blood. It probably is. There is a sea of bright blue and rich green as far as the eye can see, a roar so loud you wouldn't be able to hear your own thoughts, much less your teammates if they speak to you. They won't, though. Their eyes are too closely trained on the action on the field, to one of the greatest rivalries – cricketing or otherwise – the world has ever seen. India is facing off against Pakistan in the Champions Trophy.

India has just finished bowling in the first innings. Virat Kohli takes deep breaths as he straps on his pads in the dressing room. Across from him, he sees Rohit Sharma and Shubman

King Fit for a Kohli

Gill deep in conversation, muttering fast at each other. Strategizing. He thinks about joining them, his foot tapping relentlessly on the ground, and then thinks better of it, shaking his head and closing his eyes. He thinks, instead, of home.

He thinks of his mum, back in Gurgaon, probably watching the match on TV, all nerves and worry, to see how he does today. He thinks of Anushka, his wife, sitting in the stands, no more than a few feet away in the stadium, but might as well be on another planet for now. He thinks of his kids. He thinks of his father. He spares a quick glance around the dressing room and sees his old friends, and some new ones. *What is there but this*, he thinks to himself as he ties his shoelaces tight.

Virat hasn't had an easy time at the crease recently. The noise around him has been ever-present, loud and ceaselessly chaotic. It's been taking him longer and longer to shut it out. Sometimes he isn't able to, no matter how hard he tries. Whether his fans are telling him they love him or others are shouting from the stands that he's finished, the pressure never eases up. He feels it in his bones. He feels it in his game. The noise is so loud, sometimes it feels like it's all there is.

The roar peaks to deafening levels as Rohit and Shubman pad past Virat in the dressing room to walk onto the field. Virat catches Rohit's eye and gives him a nod, a thumbs up, for good luck. Rohit gives him a small, lopsided smile in return. Shubman looks at him with wide, determined eyes.

A wave of cheers goes up as the two opening batters walk out, bats swinging, taking a slow run-up. Virat takes a deep breath as the noise feels like it will swallow him whole. He steps up to the window of the dressing room to watch the match play out, eyes blazing, heart racing, as Rohit takes the striker's end. There's nothing to do now but wait for his turn.

Rohit is off to a strong start as he smacks away a couple of balls to the boundary. Virat thinks he might settle in after all, find his rhythm, which means Virat, third in the batting order, won't have to go in until much later. He turns away from the window just as a roar goes up. Young Shaheen Afridi had swung the ball and sent it right into the stumps, sending the bails flying with a sharp, satisfying rattle.

Virat watches Rohit walk back, head low, not in shame as much as disappointment and a little anger. India has made 31 runs and is now 1 wicket down; they need over 200 runs to win. He passes Rohit on the edge of the field; they knock fists, and then Virat, stretching slowly, languidly, like he has all the time in the world, walks onto the field to take his position at the non-striker's end.

If you were in the stands, you might think that nothing in the world could touch Virat Kohli. He looks calm, composed, determined, eyes

full of fire, wielding his bat like a sword. Virat feels his heart beating hard in his chest. For a fleeting moment, he remembers all the awful, awful days in the recent months. The first time India ever lost a Test series on its own home grounds – against New Zealand. The series in Australia when he scored a beautiful century, but it just wasn't enough.

He gives himself the walk up to the crease – only the walk up to the crease – to think about how difficult things have been recently. *What if I misjudge the ball again? What if the roar is too loud this time? What if I'm just not the player I used to be?* The moment he reaches the crease, Virat takes a deep breath, shuts out all the noise clamouring for his attention – within him, outside of him – and trains his eyes at his partner. A quiet hush falls all around him, even though the stadium is still roaring.

This is India versus Pakistan, and it's time for Virat Kohli to play some cricket.

'Whatever you want to do, do it with full passion and work really hard towards it. Don't look anywhere else. There will be a few distractions.'

– VIRAT KOHLI

2
WHERE IT ALL BEGAN

Virat has just come home with a sheaf of paper – his corrected maths test – scrunched up in his hand. He doesn't know how to explain the marks. How can he explain that the room was too hot, too stuffy, everyone was weirdly intense about the test, and Neetu ma'am had definitely not taught section C properly in class? And that the seventh-grade boys were playing cricket outside during the test, which is all he wanted to do too?

When his mother looks at the test, she doesn't seem angry. Just tired. Exasperated. 'Sit down, Virat.'

He sits obediently, with his head bowed.

'The first time you picked up that bat ...' she begins.

Virat closes his eyes.

He doesn't remember this himself, but he remembers this story told to him over and over. Sometimes it's his mum, laughing, proud, thrilled, exasperated. Sometimes it's his father, wonderingly, but with a determined glint in his eyes. Sometimes it's his sister, Bhavna, or brother, Vikas, jokingly, half-laughing, half-mocking.

Prem Kohli has just returned from a long day of work. He's a criminal lawyer, and his wife, Saroj, has been holding the fort at home. Three children, all in their own little worlds, all needing different things. She looks at him, eyes a little wild with exhaustion. 'Will you watch Virat for a little while? I have to check Bhavna's homework, and I have to make sure Vikas is still sleeping.'

Prem smiles, tired, but also happy to be back home. 'I'll watch him, just make sure Bhavna

has finished all her homework. She forgot her English assignment last time.' Saroj nods with a long-suffering sigh before calling for her daughter as she walks away. Prem turns to the little three-year-old boy on the floor, cooing softly, happily, all wide brown eyes and laughter, and his eyes crinkle with joy.

There are toys littered around him. Large toy cars, a few stuffed toys, a little red plastic bat. Prem sits cross-legged in front of his son, who giggles and starts showing him all his toys. First, a large blue toy car. Then a stuffed bear. On and on it goes until little Virat picks up the plastic bat, swinging it wildly around, all laughter and glee. Prem gently lobs a ball at him, and Virat smacks it away with a peal of laughter.

Years later, when Prem recounts that story, or Saroj tells it – when it has become a part of the Kohli family's mythology, when it has become a daily routine between father and son – they

both say they see a flicker of something bright in Virat's eyes. Like the bat was meant for him.

All the times that story is told to him – with pride, with exasperation, as a scolding, as a fact of who he is – he remembers not the bat, but the evenings with his father, who never said no to bowling to him, no matter how tired he was, no matter how late in the night it was.

The doorbell rings just as the story ends.

'Coming to play?' Seenu asks when Virat opens the door.

He looks at the bat in his friend's hand longingly. 'In a bit, yes. See you.' With all the reluctance in the world, he closes the door and goes back to sit in front of his mother.

'Who was that?' she asks a little sharply.

'Seenu,' he says truthfully. 'He was asking if I'll come down. I said no.' He works in all the contrition in the world into his voice.

Saroj sees the look in his eyes and softens a little. 'Study harder for the next test. Go.'

Virat gives her a sparkling smile as he leaps to hug her. 'Thanks, Ma! Promise, I will.' He runs out, grabbing the bat from near the shoe rack; it has been kept leaning against the wall for easy access in the event of an emergency cricket session.

This is definitely an emergency, because the two best gully cricket teams of Uttam Nagar, New Delhi – under-14 only until the older kids come to take over the ground – are battling it out on the streets. Virat's team is flailing badly by the time he gets there. Seenu glimpses him and shouts triumphantly, 'Cheeku!'

He gives him a quick rundown of how the worn, shabby tennis ball is moving on the road. Virat's brows automatically knit in concentration as he takes the crease and the lanky kid from two blocks over comes at him with the ball.

It's an easy shot, and Virat hits hard. Thus, the game begins with all the weight of an ICC Championship being played on the streets of West Delhi.

It's going well until Virat smacks a deceptively easy-looking ball with all his might. He thinks he might have hit it for a six, until he watches in horror as it blissfully sails into Aarti aunty's window with a shatter.

'Out hai!' the lanky kid – bowling again – cackles.

Virat looks up with a groan as Aarti aunty sticks her head out. *'Phir khidki tod di tune.* You've broken the window again. It's the third time this month!'

This is one of many complaints Prem and Saroj will contend with. Sometimes it's a boy's parents complaining that Virat pushed their son. 'He wasn't playing fair, Ma! Bowling three bouncers in an over is against the rules,' Virat would later defend himself. Sometimes it's a

grandmother, 'Your son doesn't leave until we send Veer down to finish the game. He has exams to study for!' When asked about it later, over dinner, Virat will say, 'He can't just bat and leave *and take the bat with him*, Papa! He has to finish the game.'

Virat plays hard, and he plays fair. He is fiercely competitive, and won't settle for anything less than the best. Cricket is serious business, and take it seriously he does. On the streets, Virat is easy enough to play with, and excellent with the bat to boot, but even the older boys are a little spooked by just how intense this nine-year-old kid can get about a match.

For Prem and Saroj, this meant a Family Meeting, and soon.

3
SALAD DAYS

Saroj sighs as she sits at the table across from her husband. It's 11 p.m., the kids are mercifully asleep, and they have sat down at the dining table with solemn faces and the determination to find a solution.

'I can't keep doing this, Prem. I can't keep having to field parents with endless complaints about our son,' Saroj begins as she slides onto the chair.

He hums, a kind of affirmation. 'The thing is, this is just who Virat is. And I can't say I think it's a bad thing. You've seen how fierce he is when he thinks someone is being unfair. This is a good thing. We should encourage it.'

They sit in silence, a kind of stalemate, until Prem clears his throat. 'What if we send him to a cricket academy? West Delhi Cricket Academy is nearby. It'll mean spending money, yes, but it'll also mean Virat can channel all his energy into actually getting good at cricket instead of breaking every window on the street.' He smiles wryly. 'It'll cost us about the same.'

The decision is made. Easily, but with the kind of careful planning any middle-class family that wants to invest in an expensive sport will have to do. Virat is thrilled when his father tells him, and for a second, Prem sees the same light in his eyes again, the one he used to get holding the little plastic bat. A week later, Virat walks into the West Delhi Cricket Academy (WDCA) holding his father's hand. It's 1998, and he has just crossed the threshold into the place that will make him who he is today.

Virat falls into the rhythm of training quickly, easily. He gets to the academy after school, runs

the drills, pads up and steps up to the nets. It's an ordinary day, like any summer day in Delhi. The sun is beating down on the grounds even as it sets in the distance. The air is hot, but every passing hour offers a little more of the blessed coolness of the evening.

Virat is batting in the nets. After the third over from a junior bowler, Virat takes off his helmet, exasperated. Rajkumar Sharma, the coach of the academy, has been watching him, all sharp eyes, from the sidelines. When he sees the boy stop, he walks to the nets with his arms raised at his sides. 'Why did you stop? Need a break?'

Virat shakes his head quickly. Too quickly. His brows are still knitted in concentration, and he's wondering how to say it, whether he should say it. His father never taught him how to back down from a fight, though, so he squares his shoulders, looks up at the coach, and says: 'The balls are too easy.'

Rajkumar Sharma doesn't react. He narrows his eyes, watching the boy. He stands erect, his brows are scrunched up in determination. He's not sure he's ever met such a serious ten-year-old. Before he can respond, tell Virat about pacing himself and working up the ranks slowly, Virat throws his head up: 'I want to face Bhaiya.' He points at the pacer three years his senior.

The boy smirks. 'Sure, sir, I'll bowl to him.'

Sharma considers dissuading them. How is he going to answer Virat's parents when they come and say their son broke his arm batting? Virat is already nodding and putting his helmet on, though, and the older boy is smiling like he's about to feast.

Sharma doesn't back off. He stands right there. Something about the fire in the boy's eyes makes him hold back from his instincts to protect him. He nods tightly at the bowler, but doesn't tell him to take it easy.

The older boy dances down and delivers the ball. Virat smacks it off to the side. On the field, that would have been a boundary. The other boys giggle. The older boy frowns, tries again, this time putting his full might behind the delivery. Virat hits it away again.

Sharma's eyes narrow. He considers chalking it up to a fluke – beginner's luck. But Virat is consistent. It happens over and over, over after over. The older boy bowls increasingly faster balls, gets more aggressive, but Virat neither shies away nor misses. The nets session ends with him holding his wicket.

The kids are relentlessly teasing the older boy. Virat takes off his helmet, shakes the sweat off of his hair. Then, he walks to the boy, holds his hand out, and as the whole ground seems to hold its breath, says: 'Well bowled, Bhaiya. I've never had this much fun batting before.'

The boy looks taken aback for a moment, and then he puts his arm around Virat. '*Kya batting*

karta hai bey.' He laughs, smacking his head lightly. Affectionately.

It feels different to Virat. On the streets, he'd be teased for showing off. Here, he's applauded for being good.

Rajkumar Sharma watches as the kids walk away, laughing, pushing each other, swarming away to find water and juice. He doesn't say much – he's never been a man of many words – but he promises himself: Virat Kohli is one to watch, and watch he will.

> '*I like to be myself, and I don't pretend. For people to connect with you, you have to be real.*'
>
> — VIRAT KOHLI

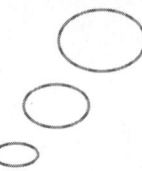

4

WHEN THE LIGHT SHIFTS

DECEMBER 2006

The wind makes the cold bite. There's no other word for it, Virat thinks to himself as he pads up in whites. The sun is watery and not all that warm – typical for a winter evening. Delhi is playing against Karnataka at the Feroz Shah Kotla, and they've been nothing short of beastly with the bat. Delhi has made 100 runs on the second day, but they're already five wickets down when Virat is called up to bat, and Karnataka has already made over 400 runs in its first innings. Catching up is going to be a tall order.

He starts slow, as he's always been taught to do. Days cricket is a long game, after all. Virat takes his place near the stumps, taps the pitch thrice with his bat as Balachandra Akhil steps up to bowl at him. He's a quick, whip-smart fast bowler, and Virat knows he'll have to be careful.

He is. Virat knocks the first ball away smartly, and takes two runs. Thus begins his innings. He's only been batting for a couple of overs when he sees the umpire squinting up at the sky. The whole field stops, holding its breath, watching the umpire. He takes the bails off the wicket, declaring the day's play closed.

Virat is pleased with himself; he's made 40 runs at a steady pace. He's less pleased about the team's standing, which is shaky right now. This is India's premier domestic tournament, the Ranji Trophy, and right now, Delhi's on shaky ground. He catches up with Ishant Sharma, his best friend on the squad. 'Four wickets man, that was some impeccable bowling,' he says easily.

He's still thinking about that great 400 on the scoreboard, though. Encouraging his teammates comes easily to him, falling behind on the field much less so.

Ishant sees this – in the distant look in his eyes, in the way he frowns when he looks down at his bat. 'We'll catch up.' He nudges his shoulder.

It's already day 2, we've made just 100. How? he thinks to himself. He looks up at Ishant and gives him a smile. 'Chhole bhature?' he asks, a mischievous glint in his eyes.

'In!' Ishant laughs.

It's fairly late into the night by the time Virat gets back home. They've had a riot of an evening. The food was excellent, the girls milling around the shop were cute, and Virat almost managed to forget how much behind Karnataka they were lagging in the match. *Almost.*

Tomorrow, we fight another day, he thinks to himself as he gets into bed.

He's woken up a few hours later, suddenly, sharply. 'Virat.' It's his mother. She sounds strangely breathless.

He sits up, alert. 'What? What happened?'

'It's your father.' Her voice is soft, and she's trying hard not to let it shake. She's mostly succeeding. 'You need to come now.'

It's late into the night, but he has no idea what time it might be. Virat feels his body go cold, and later, he'll realize it had nothing to do with the winter of the city he has called home all his life. A weird sense of foreboding sits in his chest as he makes his way to his father's room.

Prem Kohli hasn't been in the best of health recently. A stroke has left the left side of his body paralysed, but he's been doing his best to stay in the spirit of things, of life. He's been trying.

Virat knows how much his father hates depending on anyone for anything, so he expects to walk into his room to speak to him,

maybe tell him about his day batting at the crease against Karnataka, and how he's been doing well but the team's in a difficult position.

When he walks into his parents' room and looks at his father, a sinking feeling takes over his entire body, but he doesn't entirely understand why. *He looks like he's sleeping*, he thinks, a little absurdly. He turns to his mother, who's standing at the door like she doesn't want to enter the room she's been living in all these years. 'I've called for the doctors. He's cold, Virat, he's not moving, he's not responding.'

Virat doesn't remember what happens after that, not really. He remembers the calls – endless, incessant. He remembers his house filling up with family members. He remembers a doctor showing up at some point. It seems his brain registers nothing. He's still thinking about the match, about Karnataka and Delhi. It seems like another lifetime, but it's also the

only thing in Virat's life that makes sense to him at that time.

At 6 a.m., his phone rings, a wake-up call for the day's play. He has to make a decision now. His first instinct is to ask his father what he should do. It takes a moment, but reality sinks in, dully, painfully. He calls his coach, and softly, tentatively, tells him what happened, asks him what to do. When his coach asks him what he wants to do, Virat finds his reply comes easily to him: 'It doesn't feel right for me not to play, sir. That's what my father would have wanted me to do.'

Later, during the drive to the stadium, he's quiet. Virat notices his surroundings in the way one might notice birds in the sky, from a distance. Ishant sits next to him, making jokes.

Virat tries. He really tries to laugh and joke, but today, he can't find it in him, so he sits quietly and stares into the distance. When he tells Ishant what's happened, Ishant thinks he's pulling his

leg. Virat doesn't answer, but he agrees with Ishant: He doesn't believe it either; it feels like the universe is pulling his leg, playing a cruel joke on him.

He wants to tell his friend how he's feeling, but where can he find the words? It feels like the ground beneath his feet has fallen away, and he's floating in outer space with no tether. How can he explain to Ishant that the only thing that feels real right now is the grip of the bat he's holding?

Virat blinks. He wonders if he should be crying. He wonders if it's bad that he's not. He wonders if it's okay that all he wants – *needs* – right now is to get on that crease and hit the ball like his life depends on it. He feels fine until he gets to the dressing room and some of the senior players come to find him, offer their condolences, a hug, a gentle pat on his shoulder. That's when he cries. That's when it feels real: His father is gone.

When his seniors tell him not to bat, to go home, to be with his family, he has only one

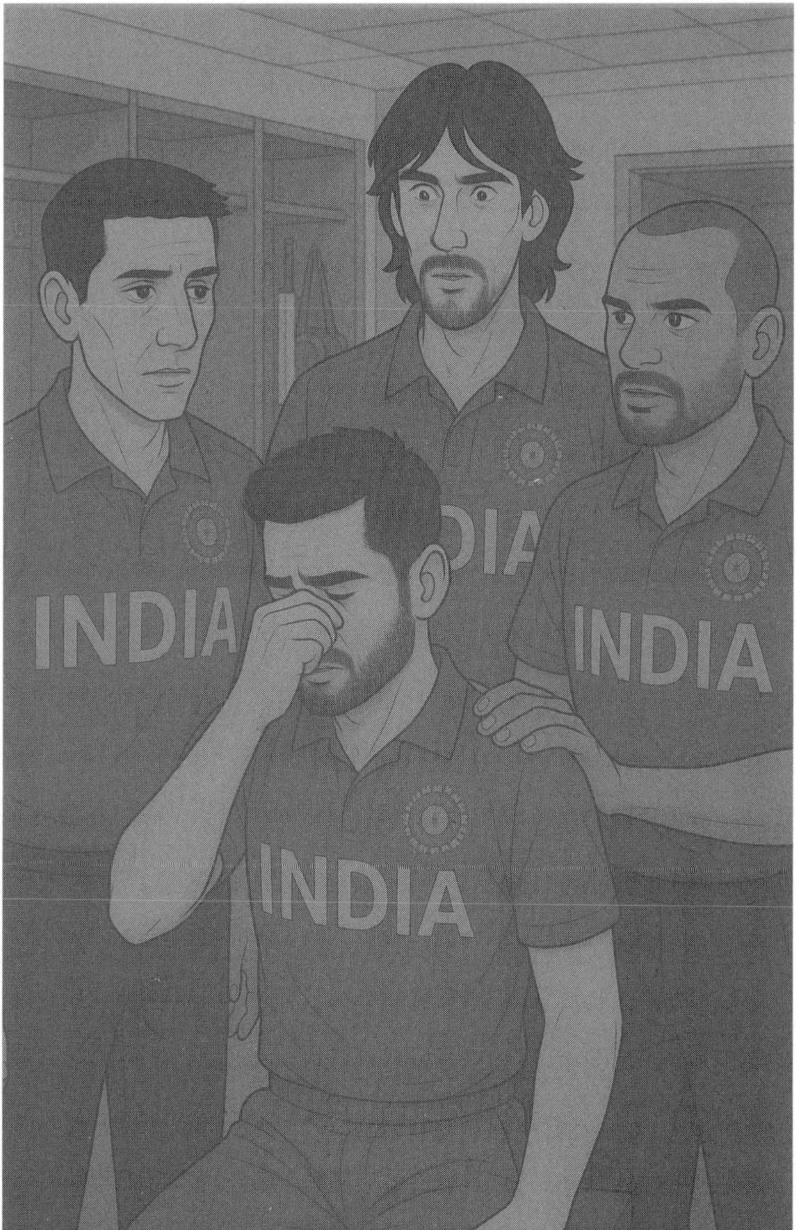
INDIA
DIA
INDIA
INDIA

answer: 'I want to bat. I want to do what has to be done.'

Virat is all focus that morning. The winter air still bites. His wrists still hurt.

But it all fades away when the Karnataka bowlers come at him. He makes 90 runs for his team before a wily ball by Balachandra Akhil gets him caught out by Thilak Naidu. Virat is sure he hasn't nicked the ball, but the umpire disagrees, and Virat must walk off.

Virat Kohli plays 238 balls in that Ranji Trophy match against Karnataka, and he scores 90 runs for Delhi. From the grounds, Virat heads straight to the cremation ground for the last rites of his father.

One day later, Delhi draw the match against Karnataka. They may not have got an outright victory – a feat unto itself in days cricket, or multi-day cricket, in India – but they did not lose. Much of that credit belongs to Virat.

'My father straightaway said, "I'm not going to pay a single penny to make him play. If he can play on his talent, so be it. If not, it's not meant to be for him." So that stuck with me for life and I've always relied on myself and what I can do as an individual first, and then I'll take help along the way.'

— VIRAT KOHLI

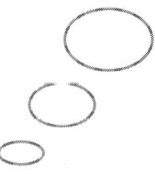

5

THE CUP OF THE WORLD

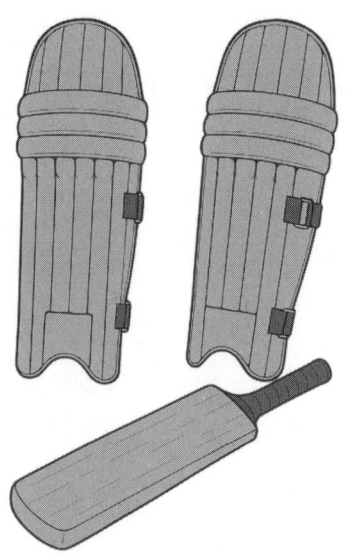

MIRPUR, 2011

Nobody expects Sachin Tendulkar to get out that quickly. India is 11 overs into the first innings. Virender Sehwag is opening with Sachin Tendulkar. Virat stands in the dressing room, eyes narrowed in focus. He's trying to get in the zone, but to be honest, he's also trying to let the fact that his name is in the playing XI sink in.

This is the 2011 Cricket World Cup, and India's squad is made up of some of its most legendary cricketers cast alongside a gaggle of newcomers, each hungry to make his mark.

The Cup of the World

Virat doesn't expect his name in the playing XI, certainly not in the first World Cup match against Bangladesh. These are, after all, cricketers he has grown up watching, idolizing. With Sachin Tendulkar and Virender Sehwag opening, and batters like M.S. Dhoni, Yuvraj Singh, Gautam Gambhir and Suresh Raina, he expects to be called up in a low-stakes match, or in case of an injury or emergency. Not in the first match of one of the biggest tournaments India is playing, where the stakes to bring the Cup home – after nearly three decades– are higher than they've ever been.

When Virat makes it to the dream list of the playing XI, the first thing he feels is a sense of disbelief. That will swirl around him all day. Closer to his heart, the second thing he feels is a weird sense of calm. It's fiery, like it's burning inside him, but it settles in his belly. He's going to do his best, he knows this in his bones.

The Cup of the World

When Sachin Tendulkar gets out in the 12th over, Virat pads up, ready to jump into the fray. He's already been told he'll be batting third, and he watches carefully as Gautam Gambhir sends the ball flying all across the field. When Gambhir is bowled in the 25th over, the stadium erupts in a roar, cheering for Bangladesh. Oddly enough, all Virat hears is silence. It's like all the noise in the stadium has receded to a distant, quiet corner of his mind. He walks to the crease, knocks gloves with Virender Sehwag – who's settled into an excellent rhythm – and gets ready to take the strike.

What follows is poetry with the bat. Virat feels a glowing sense of sharp instinct flow through him, humming in his veins. It doesn't matter who the bowler is, it doesn't matter what kind of delivery he chooses, when Virat is in the zone, he's well and truly in it. This is one of those days: His hands move before the ball comes to him;

it's like his muscles know what to do before he can even think the action through.

Sehwag is bowled. The captain, Dhoni, steps up to bat, but Virat's focus is single-mindedly trained on batting. He's vaguely aware of the score, of a milestone he's inching towards, ball by ball, but he can't think about that right now.

On the last ball of the innings, with a sharp single threaded through the fielders, Virat makes his first World Cup century in the ODI format in 83 balls, closing an innings he will never forget in his life. With this innings, Virat Kohli becomes the first Indian to score a century on World Cup debut.

The years that follow cement his place in the one-day format. He chases a terrifying target of 330 runs against Pakistan in the Asia Cup in 2012, earning him a reputation for being the go-to guy on chasing down impossible targets.

> 'A fit body gives you confidence. And there's nothing more impressive than a great attitude, which you can wear on your sleeve. But you'll have to remember the difference between being rude and being confident.'
>
> — VIRAT KOHLI

6
THE CORONATION OF CAPTAIN KOHLI

AUSTRALIA, DECEMBER 2014

This is not quite how Virat imagined he'd begin captaining Team India. M.S. Dhoni has just retired from Test cricket, and India have lost the

Border–Gavaskar series, with a draw and two victories to Australia's name. The next match is to happen at Sydney.

The battle is lost, but the match is still left to play for. The team is made up of old friends, idols he has admired and played alongside. Bringing them together, however, now falls to Virat. In his first match as the stand-in captain, he scores twin centuries. Virat almost, almost leads India to a win in the fourth innings, but the match is ultimately drawn.

Nonetheless, Virat makes his mark: He's aggressive, sharp on the field, and fully involved from the very first over. He proves himself an able captain, and a month later, in January 2015, he is made the full-time Test captain. Two years later, when Dhoni retires from limited-overs cricket, Virat takes over as captain of Team India in all the formats.

AUSTRALIA, 2018

The press conference room is buzzing – low, soft, simmering voices. Virat has been captain of the Indian cricket team for a year. He is seated at the table in the front of the room, and is asked a question about strategy, the plan for the series. His response is clear: 'Our focus is purely on our team. Obviously there will be times we'll have to put the batsman under pressure, not by crossing the line, but by getting into their heads. You expect this from any side in the world, not just Australia. No harm in a little banter.'

The jury has been out on his form as a player: 'He's at the pinnacle of cricket around the world.' 'Probably the best player in the world right now.' He rules every format as captain, and as batter.

The pressure is on. In seventy-one years, India has never won a Test series on Australian soil. The air in Australia hums a little differently.

Two of their best players have been banned for cheating, even as India are the strongest they've ever been: world-class fast bowlers, wily, sharp spinners, batters for every season, every situation, a team that's strong and sure of their strength. For the first time, everyone seems to feel it, and nobody shies away from saying it: India might sweep the Border–Gavaskar Trophy in Australia this time. Some say it will be because of the work Indian players have put in; others are less kind, announcing that India's win against a weaker Australian side shouldn't count as a *real* win.

Virat reads the news, shuffling through papers one page at a time, eyes skimming over the articles his friends and family send his way. He understands the buzz around him, but he also files it away, slowly, quietly, as noise. His focus remains singular: Play like hell, like he always does, and play to win.

THE FIRST TEST, ADELAIDE

The match is tight. Too tight. Virat feels like he never chooses to pace anymore – it's just instinct. Whether he's in the dressing room or on the field, Virat is always sharply focused, always agile, always mobile. India bat first and make a solid 250 runs, and Cheteshwar Pujara lives up to his reputation for being a wall at the crease. India's bowlers have their say, and in a match that has everyone holding their breaths, India sweep the win by 31 runs, their first in Adelaide against 2003. Virat celebrates with his teammates, but his mind is elsewhere: on the rest of the series.

THE SECOND TEST, PERTH

It's the fourth day. The sun is sweltering, the heat is legendary, and very, very Australian. Virat has been fielding in the slips. The sun beats down on his head, and the stadium is deliriously

loud. Virat has never been one to shy away from celebrating his teammates' wins – it's what makes him a beloved captain in the dressing room – so every wicket taken by his bowlers sees Virat jumping, shouting, celebrating. Virat also understands that cricket is played with the mind as much as it is played with the bat and the ball. For Virat, the strongest weapons in his arsenal are his big, loud love for the game, and his big, loud love for his team.

The Australian players understand this, too, and they, too, will do anything to win the game. Tim Paine, the Australian captain and wicket-keeper (much like M.S. Dhoni!), takes a run, but when he returns to the crease, he finds himself face to face with Virat.

'You're the one that lost it yesterday, now you're trying to be cool today,' he snipes.

The umpire has already had enough of the two captains going at each other incessantly, and he snaps at them to back off with a sharp:

'Come on, play the game. You guys are the captains.'

Both captains obey the umpire – as they must – but just as Paine is walking away, he calls to Virat: 'Keep your cool, Virat.'

Kohli hears him, and every instinct in his bones tells him to call him back, demand he repeat himself to Virat's face. Instead, he shoots a bright, dazzling smile at Paine as he walks away.

In the final innings of the Test match, when Murali Vijay steps up to bat, Paine calls to him, all smug and teasing: 'Murali, I know he's your captain – but you can't seriously like Virat as a bloke.'

The talking – also called 'chirping' or 'sledging' in cricket – is constant. Paine is constantly calling to the Indian batters and talking to them as they play, to throw them off their game. When Rohit bats, Paine calls to his bowler so everyone can hear him: 'If he hits a six here, I'm changing teams.'

The Coronation of Captain Kohli

Despite a strong fight, India lose the match to Australia. The series is now level, at 1–1, and Virat is asked about the Australian team's tactics – sledging, chirping. Virat's answer is clear: 'I'm not out here to make friends. I know my team, I know what we're capable of.'

Later, when Paine is asked about the series, he says: 'We didn't go easy on him. We thought provoking him was pointless – because that's when he plays at his best.'

THE THIRD TEST, MELBOURNE

Virat is all set to go to war with the Australian team, but as soon as he steps on the field, he finds he doesn't have to. Cheteshwar Pujara scores a spectacular century, and Jasprit Bumrah, his old friend and long-time ally on the Indian team, takes 3 wickets while only giving away 33 runs. Virat himself scores a clean 82 runs, but he finds himself truly focusing on tactics: setting the right field placements, and using his bowlers at the right time, against the right batters.

India take the win by 137 runs.

THE FOURTH TEST, SYDNEY

India post an absolutely monumental 622 runs before deciding they are ready to bowl, declaring the innings. Australia, for the first time in history, stand on the cusp of being forced into a follow-on. In Test cricket, that means the team batting second must bat again because they have fallen too far behind the team that batted first in terms of runs.

Rain saves them from further embarrassment but can't erase the result: India's first-ever Test series win in Australia. When Virat is asked about the win, he says one thing, throat closed up with emotion: 'I've never been prouder of a team. We did what no one believed we could.'

The Coronation of Captain Kohli

With this win, Virat Kohli becomes the first Indian to win a Test series in Australia – after seventy-one years, eleven tours and counting – and in that process, he oversees India's most complete overseas Test performance in decades: with dominance in batting, pace bowling and fielding. His century in the Perth Test is still remembered as one of the best of his career, against a world-class Australian attack on a pitch that was not batter-friendly in the slightest.

> 'Self-belief and hard work will always earn you success.'
>
> — VIRAT KOHLI

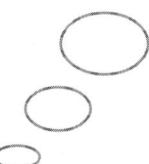

7

ONE GREAT KNOCK

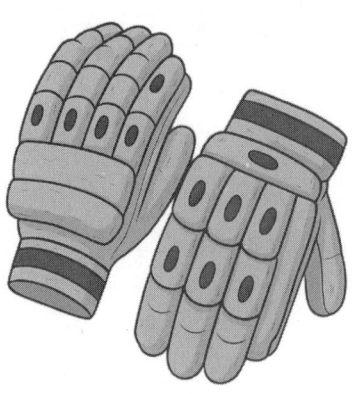

THE MELBOURNE CRICKET GROUND (MCG), AUSTRALIA, 2022

The 2022 T20 World Cup is on in Australia, and India and Pakistan are facing off against each other. India–Pakistan matches never feel like just cricket matches. Even sitting at home watching on the TV, you can feel the tension in the air like it's a solid thing. It coats the walls, settles in your lungs. It pervades both countries. Too much history, too much rage, too much riding on the result.

The first thing Virat notices when he pads up to bat for the second innings is the cold. It's freezing in Melbourne. It's easy to forget it when

One Great Knock

you're running around fielding as the opposition bats, but now that he's in the dressing room, waiting for his turn to bat, it's all he can feel. His hands shiver, his toes are cold, and he's not sure if the restlessness he feels at the tip of his nose is the temperature or his nerves.

Pakistan batted first and set India a target of 160 runs. When K.L. Rahul's wicket goes down, Virat is already padded up and ready to step up to the crease. He's not too worried. A risky wicket can happen to anyone on a bad day, but India's still got its top order raring to go, and Rohit's at the other end of the crease, all focus and determination. They knock fists quickly before Virat takes the strike.

When Rohit's caught out in the third over, a smidge of worry starts to gnaw at Virat. India has 10 runs on the board and is already 2 wickets down. He shakes it off – there's plenty more overs to go, and he knows how the long game is played.

Three overs later, that niggling sense of anxiety has become much harder to shake off. India is 4 wickets down, and Suryakumar Yadav and Axar Patel are both out of the game. When Hardik Pandya steps up, Virat doesn't say much, just taps him on the shoulder as he takes the strike. They both know where they stand, where the game stands, and how well they'll have to play to turn the tide for India.

In the 15th over, something shifts for Virat. He feels it humming under his skin, in his bones – though if asked later, he wouldn't be able to explain what changed. It feels like a fog has lifted, and he can see the game with perfect clarity, absolute sharpness. It's the kind of day when years of training come together and coalesce, and suddenly, everything you need to know, to do is already instinct and requires no thought. We all have days like that sometimes: Days that feel like they were made for us to win, to show the world what we can do.

He watches Haris Rauf take his bowling run-up, for example, and the kind of instinct only decades of training can code into you kicks in. He steps back, pivots on the back foot, and hits the ball for a six.

Virat's skin is humming with instinct, but at the end of the day, he is in control of only his own game. India makes excellent progress over the rest of the innings, but the last over is still too close for comfort. In the 19th over, when Hardik is caught out and Dinesh Karthik, the whip-smart wicket-keeper-batter from Tamil Nadu steps up, India need 16 runs off 5 balls. Virat's made 74 runs of 50 balls. The game is so tight, a clean breath feels impossible.

A no-ball, a free-hit, a five-minute argument and a planet's worth of tension later, India need 2 runs off the final ball of the match when Dinesh Karthik is run out. Virat is vaguely aware of the stillness of the Indian dugout, Rohit standing like a statue with his hands on his hips.

Ravichandran Ashwin walks up to the crease, and Virat notices how nervous he looks, how slowly he seems to be moving.

No time to think about it, he says to himself. He meets Ashwin in the middle and starts talking to him, words spilling fast out of his mouth to make sure his teammate knows how the ball is moving, where the bowler might try to bowl, what he thinks he should do. Ashwin takes the strike, and Virat feels the whole world come to a standstill.

He watches, ready to run, ready to shout, ready to fall to his knees, win or lose. What he doesn't expect at all: Nawaz, the bowler, bowls wide, and Ashwin instinctively steps away without attempting to hit it. This earns India both an extra run and an extra ball. Virat watches him in disbelief: He would have tried to hit it, but that was a terrifyingly smart thing to do.

As the final ball is bowled and his partner at the striker's end hits it away for a single run,

Virat runs at him to tackle him into a hug. The rest of the team rush onto the field to congratulate them.

India's scored a famous win, as they'll herald it later; Virat brings the team back from the brink of loss, and gives the world a cricket match they will never forget. Later, when asked about the match, Virat will say it was the best, most important innings of his life.

'When my back is against the wall, there's only one way for me and that's forward. And I will do everything in my power to fight my way up again ... So the whole journey, the kind of matches that have happened, the kind of knocks that have happened, the kind of rock bottom – when I went back home, I was like okay, I've hit rock bottom now. No one believes in me, everyone thinks I should not be playing Test cricket ... So what can I do? I can just work as hard as I can. Went into a bubble, I went to Bombay as well, I called Sachin Tendulkar, I asked for his help ... My mindset was simple. I went back home, I told myself: "Listen, you can't play Test cricket to show people that you can play in England and Australia and not get out. If you don't score it's no point. You play this game to make your team win."'

— VIRAT KOHLI

8

WHAT'S A CROWN TO A KING?

KENSINGTON OVAL, BARBADOS, 2024

India make it to the final of the ICC T20 World Cup undefeated. Virat, however, has had an underwhelming tournament run. He knows this, the world knows it, sometimes it feels like it's all anyone will ever remember about him. In seven innings, he's scored 75 runs. He's not sure anyone remembers the man who scored a century on his World Cup debut; honestly, he's not even sure *he* remembers that Virat. Young, fiery, raging. The knives of critics are sharp, their pens sharper still. The questions have been swirling for months: Is it time to retire, hang up his boots, call it a day?

Virat doesn't have answers. Not right now, not today. What he does know, what he promises himself with all his heart, is this: He will play with all his might in this T20 World Cup final. After that, let the chips fall where they may.

Rohit and Virat, old friends through the last decade of their career, pad up together, ready to open. They don't speak – an old tradition. They thump each other on the shoulder before gloving up and knocking fists. Rohit, the captain, takes the strike, while Virat takes his place at the non-striker's end.

Virat finds his rhythm quickly, but his partners are another story entirely. Just 4.3 overs in, India is 3 wickets down, with Rohit, Rishabh Pant and Suryakumar Yadav all out. The dream of bringing the World Cup home again seems more distant than ever. Virat, however, has never been one to shy away from a challenge. No matter the field, no matter the stakes, when he finds the rhythm in his movement, there's no stopping him.

This day turns out to be one of those. Kohli hits boundary after boundary, sending the ball singing, threading through the fielding placements set by South Africa. He bats for nearly 19 of the 20 overs, and scores 76 runs in 59 balls. Virat becomes the anchor of the innings, allowing India to set a solid target of 176 runs for them to defend, and for South Africa to chase. With the first innings done, however, the fielding is set by Rohit, and all Virat can do is watch and stay ready, should the ball come his way.

The team is sharp on the field, but the match is tight. It comes down to the last over, nearly the last ball. But when Hardik Pandya bowls the final ball, the stadium erupts in a deafening roar. India have won.

Virat isn't sure when the tears come; all he knows is that all his teammates are celebrating, crying, screaming, laughing. Everything seems to be happening everywhere all at once,

and Virat can't seem to find his balance. He laughs with the team, embraces his friends and colleagues without registering who's who, but when he sees Rohit, eyes red with tears, it sinks in. The scale of it, the truth of it. India has brought home an ICC Trophy again after eleven years.

After the victory lap is taken, the trophy lifted, Virat steps up, alongside Rohit and Ravindra Jadeja, to make a statement: 'This was my last T20 game playing for India.' And thus, the era of King Kohli playing T20 cricket comes to an end.

> 'In the game of cricket, a hero is a person who respects the game and does not corrupt the game.'
>
> — VIRAT KOHLI

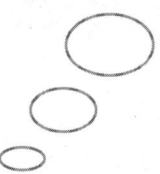

9

KOHLI FIT FOR A KING

Virat has been trying to breathe through the tight knot in his stomach. It's helped some, but the tension in the air is so thick you could cut through it. He feels it in everything: The way the crowd's roar thrums through his entire body, in the sharp gaze of Naseem Shah as he prepares to take his run-up, in the eyes narrowed in concentration over Shubman at the non-striker's end. This is the thing about cricket when the stakes are high: You know you'll only truly breathe once that last ball is bowled and you have the result in front of you.

A lot's riding on this Champions Trophy campaign for India. The world may not see it, but Virat feels it in his bones. The recent losses against New Zealand and Australia are on his mind, but he can't go there right now, will not let himself go there.

He narrows his eyes as Naseem begins his run-up for his second ball. Taps the bat against the ground twice and swings as the ball comes at him. He lifts his bat and runs, shouting for two runs, not stopping, not caring to see if the ball went for a boundary. The crowd erupts in a roar, but he doesn't stop until the umpire signals a dead ball.

When Abrar Ahmed folds his arms and nods at Shubman after his wicket, a mockingly complacent expression on his face, Virat can't help the cold fury that curls in his belly. He doesn't lose his cool, although the temptation to lean into his old ways is strong. Instinct tells him to face off with Abrar, instinct tells him to invite him to come at him like a war cry. He doesn't give in to it.

In all his time in love with cricket, Virat has learned that the game will test many things about you: your determination, your sense of self, your ability to take losses on the chin; sometimes it tests your patience, your calm on the field; at others, it tests your ability to fight back, to show you mean business. The rewards are great, he knows this, but the costs are too. Ask any cricketer who comes home after a difficult loss to a world that seems to have turned against them.

Virat doesn't give in to his instinct to fight Abrar; he focuses on the ball instead. It rewards him, and well: He makes a century off 111 balls, and helps India to a beautiful six-wicket win against Pakistan, their oldest rivals.

When he lifts his helmet to celebrate, he'll discover that his innings have made him the fastest to ever make 14,000 runs in the ODI format, even faster than the legendary Sachin Tendulkar. Later, much later, when he allows himself to watch the match highlights again,

he'll hear the commentator Harsha Bhogle call it 'another jewel in the King's crown', and he will think of victory, but also of how hard it has been to get here.

> *'On the field, aggression can sometimes be a positive emotion. It boosts performance and can lift your game. But over the years, I have learnt that restrained aggression is a better animal.'*
>
> — VIRAT KOHLI

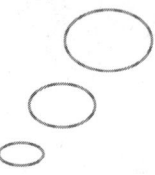

10

VIRAT KOHLI: THE MAN

Virat Kohli is married to the famous Bollywood actress Anushka Sharma. Virat and Anushka met while shooting an advertisement for a shampoo and fell in love. They have two kids, and now live in London. They love hanging out together, and Anushka often comes to cheer for him during his matches.

Virat is very close to his mother, who used to be big on making sure he ate dal instead of butter chicken. He says she still gets sad and teary-eyed when he's playing badly.

Virat is also called 'Cheeku' – he acquired the name after his first coach saw his chubby cheeks as a child and started calling him Cheeku after the rabbit in *Champak* magazine.

Virat's favourite things to eat are butter chicken and chhole bhature, and he's vocally said he's a big fan of Delhi's legendary street food.

Since 2011, however, he's been a vegan – he says it has greatly helped his energy levels. He's particularly fond of quinoa and spinach, and loves drinking smoothies for breakfast.

Virat loves going to the gym, and his bookshelf is full of philosophical self-help books. He's also a big believer in spirituality.

Virat's favourite video game is FIFA, and he's previously said he used to play it a lot.

Virat is known for his sharp sense of fashion and his love for cars. There's a famous story of him wanting to be the ambassador of Audi, so he started driving their cars. Guess who's the ambassador of Audi now?

He owns a fashion line called WROGN – spelled exactly like that – and runs a foundation

that supports underprivileged children. He makes sure kids who can't afford to enter the world of sports can get opportunities.

Virat is close friends with Ishant Sharma, who used to play with him for Delhi. He's also good friends with A.B. de Villiers, K.L. Rahul and Rohit Sharma. He looks up to M.S. Dhoni – who was his first captain, under whom he made his international debut.

Virat also sometimes talks to his bat when he's playing.

Virat is a huge fitness nerd. When he was younger, he used to party a lot and eat whatever he wanted to. In 2012, he had a turning point where he realized: 'This isn't who I want to be.' He would later say: 'I looked at myself in the mirror and said – you can't look like that if you want to be the best in the world.' He became a vegetarian a few years later, and more recently went vegan.

11
EPILOGUE

2025

Virat Kohli has always had a special relationship with the number eighteen. He has worn it on his jersey his entire life. His father passed away on 18 December in 2006; he made his debut for India on 18 August 2008.

Eighteen years is how long Virat Kohli has been part of the Royal Challengers Bengaluru (RCB) Indian Premier League (IPL) team. He was nineteen years old when the auction hammer went down on him in the first-ever IPL auction. He's worn the RCB red his entire adult life. And he's come close, so close to lifting the trophy of the world's largest, most famed cricket league. The IPL's nearly man, they call him; '*Ee saala cup namde*, this year the cup will be ours', they tease him.

It's been a long year six months into 2025, a long IPL season. Virat has retired from Test cricket after his final away series in Australia. He's been having a strong run at home in the IPL.

When the final against Punjab Kings rolls around, the battle is between two teams who have never won the IPL before. Virat is well prepared. He thinks, truly, really believes, he is also prepared for any outcome emotionally.

When the last ball is bowled, and RCB win the IPL after almost-but-not-quite-never-fully winning for eighteen years, Virat finds he's not prepared after all. His throat closes up, his eyes blur with tears, and he buries his face in his hands as the crowd erupts into a deafening roar.

Later, he will say: 'I've given this team my youth, my prime, and my experience, I've tried

to win this every season, giving it everything I have. To finally have this moment come … it's an unbelievable feeling.' Later, he will call it one of the greatest achievements of his career, one of the most important victories of his life. Later, when he finds Anushka in the stands and buries his face in her shoulder and falls apart weeping, he will think: 'This has all been worth it.'

'I have had a lot of moments where I really, really doubted myself and had to recalibrate and find a way to slowly build up again ... Whenever I entered the ground for practice or for the Test match I just kept telling myself that ... that thought came to me very naturally. So yeah, that's when you believe that there is a certain power up there, which, if you're honest towards what you're doing, you'll always be shown the way ...'

— VIRAT KOHLI

VIRAT KOHLI: THE FACT FILE

LET'S TALK MILESTONES

Some very cool milestones Virat Kohli has achieved in his career include scoring a century across both innings of a Test match. He's also made a century in one innings of a Test match and gotten out for zero – also called a duck – in a Test Match. In the Test and ODI formats, he has the impressive achievement of having taken 50 catches – also called fielding dismissals – and scoring 5,000 runs in the format. In the ODI format, Virat has had the bad luck of being dismissed right before a century (at 99 runs!) the most times.

TEST FORMAT

123 MATCHES

55.57 STRIKE RATE

210 INNINGS

30 CENTURIES

13 NOT OUTS

31 HALF-CENTURIES

9230 RUNS

30 SIXES

254* HIGHEST SCORE

1027 FOURS

46.85 AVERAGE SCORE

121 CATCHES

ODI FORMAT

- **302** MATCHES
- **93.34** STRIKE RATE
- **290** INNINGS
- **51** CENTURIES
- **45** NOT OUTS
- **74** HALF-CENTURIES
- **14181** RUNS
- **152** SIXES
- **183** HIGHEST SCORE
- **1325** FOURS
- **57.88** AVERAGE SCORE
- **161** CATCHES

T20I FORMAT

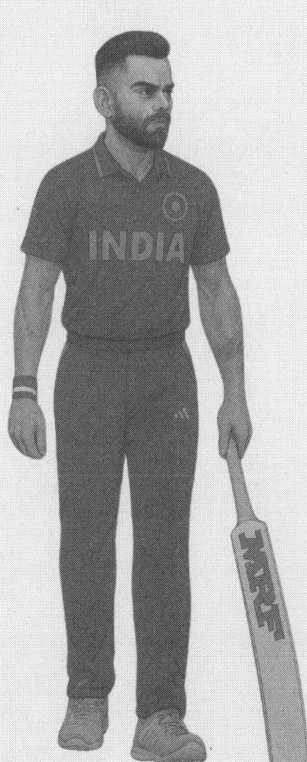

125 MATCHES	**137.04** STRIKE RATE
117 INNINGS	**1** CENTURIES
31 NOT OUTS	**38** HALF-CENTURIES
4188 RUNS	**124** SIXES
122* HIGHEST SCORE	**369** FOURS
48.69 AVERAGE SCORE	**54** CATCHES

IPL FORMAT

ROYAL CHALLENGERS BANGALORE

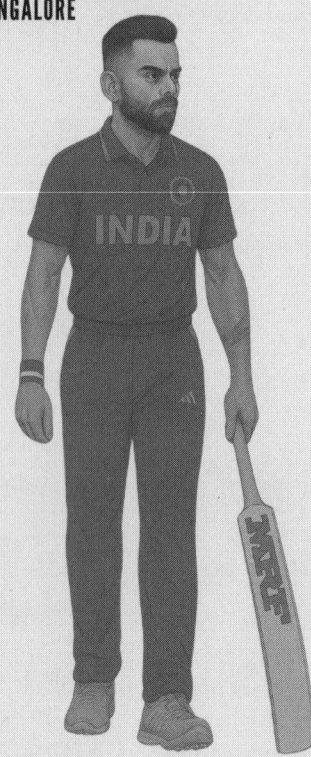

- 267 MATCHES
- 132.85 STRIKE RATE
- 259 INNINGS
- 8 CENTURIES
- 40 NOT OUTS
- 63 HALF-CENTURIES
- 8661 RUNS
- 291 SIXES
- 113* HIGHEST SCORE
- 771 FOURS
- 39.54 AVERAGE SCORE
- 117 CATCHES

FEATS

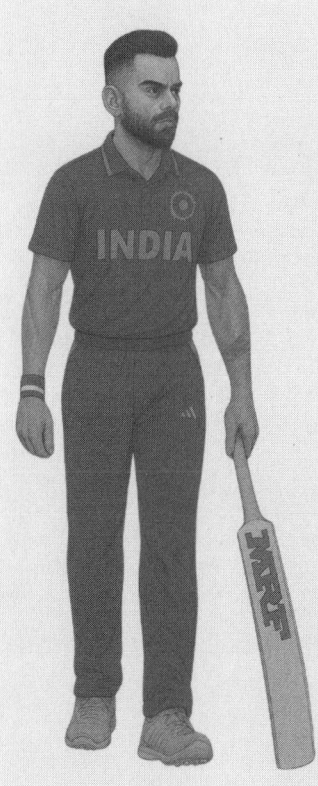

FEAT	VALUE
MOST HUNDREDS AGAINST ONE TEAM - ODI	SRI LANKA
MOST FIFTIES IN A CAREER - T20I	39
MOST PLAYER OF THE SERIES AWARDS - T20I	7
MOST PLAYER OF THE SERIES AWARDS - TEST, ODI, T20I	21
FASTEST TO 3,500 RUNS - T20I	96
FASTEST TO 14,000 RUNS - ODI	287
SECOND MOST PLAYER OF THE SERIES AWARDS - ODI	11
SECOND MOST FIFTIES IN CAREER - ODI	125
SECOND MOST HUNDREDS IN A CALENDAR YEAR - TEST, ODI, T20I	637

OTHER BOOKS IN THE SERIES

You need unshakeable belief to be a champion, no matter where you come from. From growing up as a poor kid whose family couldn't afford his coaching to smashing world records, Rohit's journey has been full of never-give-up moments. Follow him through his school days, his ups and downs, the epic captaincy wins and, of course, the super-duper, totally amazing World Cup. Here's a warning: once you start reading this book, you may just not be able to stop.

Once upon a cricket field, there was a boy named Shubman who loved nothing more than hitting the ball out of the park. In 2018, he helped India win the U19 World Cup and was crowned the best player of the tournament. Just a few years later, he would smash a record-breaking double century in ODIs – becoming the youngest Indian to do so. Now 25, and India's Test and ODI captain, he leads the team he once only dreamed of being a part of. Here's a warning: once you start reading this book, you may just not be able to stop.